Eternal Never Ending Now

Janet Kuypers

Cyberwit.net
HIG 45 Kaushambi Kunj, Kalindipuram
Allahabad - 211011 (U.P.) India
http://www.cyberwit.net
Tel: +(91) 9415091004
E-mail: info@cyberwit.net

Printed at Repro India Limited.

Contents

Our Color, Our Gender, Our Creed

There is a house inside of me.
It's a house with a rich heritage
brimming with the knowledge
of how our souls have flourished,
and about how it all can be so quickly taken away.

There is a house inside of me
that has had to shut down
to hide everything away, because
those who didn't look like me
decided that I was nothing, and treated me accordingly.

There is a house inside of me.
It's pulse has an infectious rhythm
that we've had to stifle, to hide from
your generic white bread world; we only
let it out when we're alone, to save us from your madness.

There is a house inside of me.
I've hidden it away, I've sealed it up
and placed it deep within, brimming
with my history *and* my future, and I
don't let it out when people can't think of me as human.

There is a house inside of me.
I've put boards over the windows
to save myself from your storm.
With your wrath, I've learned to
not fight back — only because my captor won't listen.

There is a house inside of me.
And this house will stand strong
even after you have raped me,
beaten me, tortured me, tried to
kill me, treated me as nothing. But you were *so* wrong.

There is a house inside of me.
And what you don't realize is that
this house will outlast yours. Trust me.
If your house was built on distrust
and such blatant disrespect, your house is bound to collapse.

Because after all this time, and after
my *wanting* to fight, I have learned
that passive resistance is only part of
my story. Because in these struggles
I have gained a wisdom and a connection that is beyond

this house inside of me, beyond
this sharing, this inquisitive mentality.
So I want you to remember, this house
is a symbol for all like me, and for those
not like me too. Because, I have a dream that everyone

who has suffered like this — and even
those who have not — should *share*
their stories with all of the world,
no matter our color, our gender, our creed.
This is my dream. Because *this* is how we truly grow.

(this poem was written on Martin Luther King, Jr. day)

Last Before Extinction

Now he has so many opportunities.
He has nothing to lose. Why not
come out of the wilderness, attack
everything it sees. Kill something.
Suck the blood out, make him feel
alive for once more. Let them try
to restrain him. He has nothing to lose.

And for now it can fly to the highest
redwood, look out over the world.
Despise the world, the world that made
him be alone, leaving him alone. Who
will carry his name? Who will care
for him when he is old? Who can he
read bed time stories to?

Now it can feel death creeping upon
him, closer and closer. He wants to
scream. He calls upon nature; the
tides rise, earthquakes shatter homes.
He does not feel vindicated. He has lost.

And for now she can swim to the deepest
darkest cave in the Pacific, hide from
the solitude, swim lower and lower;
can she find where all of the other
animals of dying species hide, can she
find them. There must be others. They
can understand, they can live together,
at the bottom of the earth. Could they
show their pain for their species, share
what is left of their love, create a new race?

Soon they will be no more
and we will be taking their bones,
reassembling them, studying their
form, rebuilding their lives, revering
them more than we ever did
in life. This is what it all becomes.
This is what it all boils down to.
Study the bones. Study the mistakes.
Study the bones.

Everything Was Alive And Dying

(12/8/19 studio TV show recording)

I had a dream the other night
I walked out of the city
to a forest
and there were neatly paved bicycle paths
and trash cans every fifty feet
and trash every ten

as I walked, there was a stray cat
she still had her little neon collar on
with a little bell
and she walked a few feet,
stretched her front paws,
oh, she looked so darling
and then she walked right up to me
and she said thank you
and I said for what?
And she just looked at me for a moment,
her little ears were standing straight up,
and then she said, you know,
in some countries I'm considered a delicacy.
And I said how do you know of these things?
And she said,
when somebody eats one of you
word gets around
and then she looked up at me again
and said, and in some countries
the cow is sacred. Wouldn't they

love to see how you humans
prepare them for slaughter,
how you hang them upside-down
and slit their throats
so their still beating hearts
will drain out all the blood for you
and she said isn't it funny
how arbitrary your decision
to eat meat is?
and I said, don't put me
in that category, I don't eat meat
and she said I know

and I woke up in a sweat

so tell me, Ted Canadian Cuban Cruz
so tell me, Nancy my eyes are pried open Pelosi
so tell me, Mitch the slowest turtle McConnell
so tell me, Crooked Hillary Clinton
so tell me, Entertainer in Chief Donald Trump
so tell me, Barrack Hussein Obama
if you woke up from that dream
would you be in a sweat, too?

Because everything is linked here
we destroy our animals
so we can be wasteful and violent
we destroy our plants
we destroy our earth
we're even destroying our air
we wreak havoc on the soil, on the atmosphere
we dump our wastes into our lakes
we pump aerosol cans and exhaust pipes

and you think I'm extreme?

so I'm beginning to think
that we just keep doing it
because we don't know how to stop
and deep inside we feel the pain of
all that we've killed
and we try to control it by
popping a chemical-filled pain-killer

we live through the guilt
by taking caffeine, nicotine, morphine
and we keep ourselves thin with saccharin
and we keep ourselves sane with our alcohol poisoning

the thing is, in the wild
you have no power over anyone else

now that we're "civilized"
we create our own wild

maybe when we have all this power
the only choice we have
is to destroy ourselves

and so we do

Vegetarian Stands by the Meat Sale

it's raining out,
and no one wants to be outside.
and if they *do* come here,
they just want to get the bare essentials
and get home as quickly as they can.
they surely don't want to contend
with *me,* just trying to make a living.

a huge clock looms at the opposite wall.
i keep glancing at the time, and think
of the huge calendar looking over new york
in *Atlas Shrugged,* as everyone is reduced
to merely trudging through their days.

someone just wished me good luck,
because i think everyone would rather be
sleeping than here. and it's true.

i just glanced at that clock again.
i'm only one eighth the way
through my day. and this woman
who has chosen to not have children
has to keep smiling despite the weather
and fawn over every passing child i see.
this vegetarian stands next to the sign
saying "hot ham" is the deli sale today,
as employees place baked and fried chicken
in packages for sale behind me.
i try to smile, because it's my job,
even though it's raining outside,
as the second hand on the clock clicks
more slowly today.

On a High Horse Like This

I listened to a hunter from Africa
say
"all life is sacred"

and he said that after separating
a small, thin, non-venomous snake
from around a large African hawk-like bird's neck

because you see, the bird attacks snakes,
but that snake couldn't eat the large bird once it died:
that would have been a senseless death.

"all life is sacred," you say.
so I couldn't help but think:
as a hunter, do you pray for the sacred dead

after you killed it?

I mean, I don't usually vocalize
when I'm on a high horse like this

and I've had to explain myself
to meat eaters:
no these aren't leather shoes

I wear; I'm a vegetarian.
though I still have to feign a smile
to commiserate with men eating slaughtered

animal. cause you see, I'd look like a fool
for having beliefs. people don't want to hear about
a moral choice different from their own.

I mean, we're Americans,
if it's not human,
or maybe a dog or a cat, eat it. it's that simple.

###

but I married a hunter
a marine who served our country
and he told me

that every time he killed an animal
a part of him felt a regretful twinge of pain
when he killed his prey.

the prey that *he* searched for.
with a weapon he could use
before anything got close enough

to be an enemy.

oh, I'm sorry.
I'm getting on my high horse again.

it's convenient that people
can get their kill from the grocery store
without getting any blood

on their hands.
anything to stop everyone from thinking
about what they're doing.

because I've heard that killing something
makes you feel something.
And I thought:

Original Snowbirds

I'd like to tell you a story about a bird.
It's fair to say this is the original snowbird.

In Hawaii, the Kolea is the Pacific Golden Plover.
These foraging birds hang out in Hawaii

until it is spring, where they've fattened up
for their over 2,000 mile nonstop flight to Alaska.

They have no waterproofing on their feathers,
so they don't rest, but fly for 3 days straight.

And fossils found on Oahu even reveal
that plovers have done this 120,000 years.

Because in the spring, they fly up north,
and these birds spend three months in Alaska.

They reclaim last year's breeding grounds
and incubate eggs, hatching in 25 days.

Momma and daddy bird leave the nest
just after the last chick hatches —

and predators like foxes, Jaegers & caribou
force the chicks to leave the nest.

In barely a month the chicks can then fly,
come August, which is when the parents then leave.

Now, these adult Plovers eat like mad,
gain 50% of their body fat

so they have fuel for their 3 day flight —
over 2,000 miles — to their Hawaiian home.

Yeah, you heard me right, every spring
these Pacific Golden Plovers, after bulking up,

make a 3 day nonstop flight up north
and lose 50% of their body mass doing it.

And right after their babies are ready to fly
and they've bulked up enough once more

they leave their babies to fend for themselves,
'cuz these little ones can't make the flight:

they don't have the bulk to make the trip
and they never even learned how to navigate.

With Alaska summers they'll never see stars —
or a night sky at all — until they fly south.

Maybe baby Plovers use earth's magnetic field,
'cuz it's a miracle when they do reach Hawaii.

But I've been told that when they return,
they arrive in Hawaii at the exact same spot,

year after year, for up to 20 years, and
annually are welcomed by the natives.

We think we understand the seasons.
But in Hawaii they mark the seasons

by the coming and going of the Kolea,
the Hawaiian word that mimics the sounds

of the Pacific Golden Plovers, the parents and
their babies, 'cuz they mark the passage of time.

Unique Noise

I have shared my call with the world.
For those close, who listened,
they responded.
So I shared.
And we
were
happy.

Now I have stepped onto foreign soil
and suddenly I feel so alone.
There is suddenly no one
for me to call to.
I am lost, with
no chance
for me to
share my
soul.

#

I recently heard of a lonesome whale
in the Pacific. His mating call
is 52 Hertz, which is
higher than
any whale
can
hear.

Navy researchers studied this one noise,
this one unique noise, for years,
and as far as they
could tell,
only one
whale
made
this
call.

And I've been pacing my apartment,
thinking about this one lost whale.
Wondering, are they
lonely. Are they
bound to be
this way
forever.

#

And I think I'm beginning to understand
that pit in your stomach feeling,
that loneliness that won't
go away because
when you look
around, you
see no
one.

And I want to swim to the deepest depths
of the Pacific, look for who is lost,
they have to be there somewhere,
let me find them. Let me
tell them they're
not alone,
even if
I
am.

But I know this is all a useless battle,
if I found them, they wouldn't hear me,
I wouldn't be able
to help. And we
would remain
together,
but
alone.

Because now that I am on foreign soil
I've forgotten how to stretch
my hand, hoping someone
will want to take it.
So I stand here,
far too alone,
and far too
frightened
to feel
free.

Eternal Never Ending Now

We struggle in our worlds
we contend with regular problems
and we look for relief

in any way we can. We
think a vacation can temporarily
assuage how we feel,

and it does, and then
it is back to the same old grind, the
same never ending

meaninglessness. I know
it's hard, I know it seems hopeless,
but I want to ask you:

can you take a moment;
can you pause and think of a time
in your life, any time,

when you felt at peace.
It may have seemed a lifetime ago.
Maybe it was at a beach

at sundown, listening to
the waves crash. Maybe it was sitting
along a mountainside,

watching the little cars
driving down the little roads below.
Maybe it was jumping

in a vat of fresh soybeans
when the farmer says to look around
the farm, and all you smell

is fresh wheat, and dew
on all the lush green around you. I won't
bring up references to

bubble baths or baseball
games. Just think back to what works
for you. And remember it.

And what I want you to do
is find that moment, and you may realize
that time then seemed

to stand still. There was
no past, there was no future, there was
just an eternal, never ending

now that didn't end. During
that moment, you don't even remember
it ending, it was that complete.

If you can remember those
times, if you can reflect on those times,
then know that the perfect

moment of completeness,
of wholeness, is within you, Find it. Know
that peace is with you always.

Vanishing Scars

"They tell you how it was...
and how it happened
again and again. They tell
the slant life takes when it turns
and slashes your face as a friend."
        — William Stafford, from "Scars"

Any wound is real, he says,
and yes, it's true, I know it.[*]
For *the faces of promise*
are also the *places*
the scars will be.

Yes, bright-eyed children,
this is the battle
you have to look forward to.
Brace yourself,
if you know how.
It might hurt less then.

For once we are grown
we are all too aware
of past tortures and traumas,
they leave physical and emotional scars
we wear like badges,
while knowing
these scars
scar us.

Hide the marks from your face,
your stomach from when
you were hospitalized
against your will for months.
Hide the bruises around your neck
as you leave the country
to escape the man
who once claimed he loved you.
Force yourself to forget
the disappointing diatribes
your disappointment of a father
gave you, while you struggle
to be stronger than him,
despite him.

If you internalize some scars,
turn them around,
then watch your helplessness
transform to rage,
then to solace and insight
to help others recover
from their own physical
and sexual traumas.

They say that time heals all wounds,
and you wish for the scars to vanish;
your brutish, broodish demeanor
is a blemish
              you wish would perish —

but wait a minute,
search for that scar
on the cleft of your chin
from when you scratched
when you had the Chickenpox.
You would swear
that scar was there,
but

where did it go.

Then you turn
to the one you love.
They tell you
they've never seen the scars.

That you've always been
a bright white beam of light,
almost too blinding
for anyone to fully take in,
which is why
you can never
be fully understood...
And this is all they think
when they see you,
and all they can say
is
I love you.

And maybe that
is the treatment
for the traumas...

and the scars
too hard
to handle.

Any wound is real,
for scars too hard to handle.
And *any wound is real,*
as long as you give it the power
to take over your soul
and fester into a fiendish demon.

So just remember
that despite those vanishing scars
that are now
too taxing to tally,
despite those battle scars...

you are a blinding light
that no one,
thankfully,
will ever
fully
understand.

Italicized portion of this poem are quotes from the William Stafford poem "Scars".
* line toward the end of the Ai poem "The Good Shepherd: Atlanta, 1981."

X-raying Metal Under my Skin

Went to a back doctor
where chiropractors twisted my back,
heard strings of cracks along my spine
at every appointment —

and at one point
they took an x-ray of my chest and back,
checking for disc injuries and inspecting
the curve of my spine.

Went into the office,
they bought me into a room, turned a light box
on at the wall, placed my x-ray in the light
and asked,

"What is this?",
and they pointed at what almost looked
like an angular spider missing a few legs
in one of my veins.

I started for a moment.
Then I think my eyes turned into saucers
when I realized what this foreign object was
in my body.

"Oh, that's a
Vena Cava filter," I said to them. "It was
placed in me when I was in a coma
and they didn't know

when I'd wake up."
They looked at me for a second, 'til I said,
"I've always wondered what that looked like."
And although

it's metal in my vein
that would vibrate, tear through the veins
to my heart and instantly kill me if I ever
had an MRI scan,

although this metal
was placed in my vein without my consent
when I was in a coma, despite this, I
wanted this x-ray

so I could feel
some sort of connection to this invader.
I know, I know, it's only there to stop
blood clots

from traveling
to my heart or lungs or brain that would
kill me, I know it's only there to help, but
this foreign object

has taunted me
for too many years now, planting seeds
of distrust in the back of my mind. This
microscopic monster

was placed in my vein,
driving this love/hate relationship I now have
to this non-human object embedded
deep inside me.

I know it's there.
At times I think I can feel it. I think this metal
mini spider is also scratching at my soul,
to remind me

that something foreign
has invaded me, I can't claw it away, and while
I hate it *and* I need it, it always reminds me
that there is something

deep inside me
that will invade me like this
forever.

I'm not sick but I'm not well

I'm not sick but I'm not well
and I'm sure there's something I can do about this
I've popped the aspirin
        the tylenol
        the ibuprofen
        the codine
        the prozac
        the sleeping pills
and that thermometer is down my throat
and I'm gagging

I'm not sick but I'm not well
the doctors find nothing wrong with me
and believe me, they've taken the x-rays
they've striped me down
and made me wear one of those awful paper robes
and they've felt me up
and checked me out
and found what they were looking for
but didn't find anything I was looking for

I'm not sick but I'm not well
and I can't help but think
that everything I'm doing to make things better
might only be making things worse
so I don't want to listen to what
you have to say anymore

and I want this IV out of my arm
and I want this oxygen tube out from my nose
and I want this suppository out of my ass
and I want you to get that scalpel away from me
because I want everything I've got

I'm not sick but I'm not well
and they want me if they can keep me in line
and they want me if they can cut me open
        and take out my insides
        and suck out the fat
        and suck out the life
        and make me generic
        and make me dependent
        make me unreal
        make me not whole
and I've walked that line with all you doctors
and I want all my parts back
and I want to be healthy

no, I'm not sick and maybe I'm not well
but you're only making me worse
I don't have the answers but neither do you
so instead of tearing me apart
        and dissecting me
        and studying the bones
let me just stay together for a while
until I figure it all out

Fantastic Car Crash

and our life is one big road trip now
and we set the cruise control
and make our way down the expressway.

and most of the time we're just moving
in a straight line, and the scenery
blurs. there's nothing to see

but I know what's inside you and I
know what you're made of. I know
there's no such thing as a calm with you

you are a fantastic car crash. you stop
traffic in both directions as the gapers gawk and
the delay grows and they slow down and stare

everything shatters with you, you know.
it's a spectacular explosion. I try
to duck and cover as metal flies

through the air. and every time you leave
the scene of the accident
I am left picking up the shards of glass

from the windows. you know, the glass breaks
into such tiny little pieces. they look like
ice. it takes so long to pick up the pieces

even though I'm careful
I'm still picking up the pieces
and I'm still on my knees

and the glass cuts into my hands
and the blood drips down to the street.
think of it as my contribution

to this fantastic car crash
that is you, that is me, that is us
as I pull the glass from my hands

and I wave my hand to the line of traffic:
go ahead, keep driving, this happens
all the time, there's nothing to see here

Right There, By Your Heart

(verses 2 and 6)

have you ever had that feeling before, you
know, the one when someone is telling
you something you don't want to hear, like
if someone was about to tell you that someone
died and you knew what they were going to say
and you still didn't want to hear it, or if
someone did something to you you didn't like,
like when you were little and the kids at the
bus stop shot pebbles and spit balls at you every
day because you were smart and you still had
to go to the bus stop every morning and just
try to ignore them? and when that happens
it feels like a medium sized rock just fell
into the bottom of your stomach, and you
don't want to move because you're afraid
that the rock will hurt the inside of your stomach
and so you just have to sit there and hope
the rock goes away? or else you get the feeling
in your chest, right between your lungs, it feels
like someone is pressing against the bone there,
right there by your heart, and you've got to
breathe, you're not going to be able to take
that pressure, that force any longer?

—

i don't know how many times the idea of seeing him
went through my mind. at least once a week i'd imagine
a scene where he'd confront me, and i'd somehow
be able to fight him back, to show him that he didn't
bother me any more, to show him that the rock wasn't
there any more. to somehow be able to prove that
i wasn't a victim any more. i was a survivor. that's
what they call it now, you see, survivor, because
victim sounds too trying for someone who has been
raped. so i keep saying i'm over it but i keep imagining
mark all over again, not raping me, but following me
on the street, coming to my door with flowers, or
sending me a valentine. but once, when i saw him
walking out of a record store as i was walking in, the
rock fell so hard that i thought i was going to be sick
right there by the cash register, right there by those
metal things at the doorway that beep when you
try to take merchandise out of the store, you know
what those things are, i just can't think of what
they're called. but if i did that, then he'd know he was still
winning, to this day. how many years has it been? how
many years since he did that to me? how many years
since i've been wanting to fight him, since i've been
feeling that rock in my god-damned stomach?
i managed to hide my face from him in the store so he
didn't see me as he walked out. when i saw he was
gone, i wondered why i still felt the pressure in my
chest. i thought the pressure was going to turn
my body inside-out. i reached for my heart, grabbed
at my shirt. maybe the pain was always there, right there,
by my heart, but i try not to think of it until i
go through times like those.

the Burning

I take the final swig of vodka
feel it burn it's way down my throat
hiss at it scorching my tongue
and reach for the bottle to pour myself another.
I think of how my tonsils scream
every time I let the alcohol rape me.
Then I look down at my hands —
shaking — holding the glass of poison —
and think of how these were the hands
that should have pushed you away from me.
But didn't. And I keep wondering
why I took your hell, took your poison.
I remember how you burned your way
through me. You corrupted me
from the inside out, and I kept coming back.
I let you infect me, and now you've
burned a hole through me. I hated it.
Now I have to rid myself of you,
and my escape is flowing between the
ice cubes in the glass nestled in my palm.
But I have to drink more. The burning
doesn't last as long as you do.

Women's Very Existence

rape is neither a sex crime
or a crime of passion

rape is not an isolated brutal crime
against women

rape is often premeditated
rape is a crime of violence
rather than sex
it is a crime of violence
against women

it is an attack by men
on women's bodies
on women's feelings
on women's very existence
                    Bob Lamm, 1976

i still have to take showers a lot. i mean,
every once in a while, no matter how clean
i am to the rest of the world, i have to go
take a shower. i lock all the doors, i close
the shades on the windows, i put a towel
over the bathroom mirror. turn the water on,
piping hot, so steam is billowing out of
the bath tub. i finally undress, open the
curtain, put my foot in, burn my foot with
the water. i wish i could hold my foot there,
just a little longer. i turn down the water.
wait for it to cool down, then step in. then
i just put my head under the shower head. hold
it there for a while. catch my breath. get the
soap. start scrubbing. i use the soap first,
then i get the bath brush. scrub off a layer
of skin. i know this makes no sense. my skin
is red, from the heat, from the scrubbing.
but i know i'm still not getting it off, it's
down there, the molecules are embedded
deep inside of me, and i'll have to rip my skin
off, pull out my organs before it goes away.
but for now all i can do is take showers.

White Knuckled

The hot air was sticking
to her skin   almost pulling
tugging at her very
flesh   as she walked
outside   down the
stairs from the train
station. Just then a
breeze hot and
sticky   hit her
in just the wrong
way, brushed against her
lower neck, and she
felt his breath again,
not his breath
when he raped
her, but his   stench
hot   rank
when he was
just close to her.
Her breath quickened,
like the catch of her
breath when she has
just stopped
crying.

All the emotion
is still there   not
going away. She
walks to the bottom
of the stairs, railing
white-knuckled by her
small tender hands;
the hands of a child,
and that ninety degree
breeze suddenly
gives her a
chill. They say when
you get a chill it means
a goose walked
over your grave.
She knows better. She knows
that it is him
walking, and that
he trapped that child in
that grave

Thank You, Women who Work *(I)*

Thank you, women who work
In this way you make
an indispensable contribution
to the growth of a culture
which unites reason and feeling,
to a model of life ever open
to the sense of "mystery"
> *Letter to Women, Message of His Holiness*
> *POPE JOHN PAUL II, July 10*

Thank you, women who work
because you take on the responsibilities of men
while still having to be mothers, wives
good little daughters a feminine creatures

Thank you, women who work
because you are the ones we can blame
when the family falls apart

Thank you, women who work
because you make a point to do more
than your fair share
even though
no man would do the same for you

Thank you, women who work
for you know you have to prove yourselves
over and over and over again

and that it still isn't enough, so
keep up the good work,

ladies

Burn It In *(reaching the end edit)*

Once I was at a beach
off the west coast of Florida
with a friend on New Year's eve.
I watched the waves crash
as the yellow moon hung over the gulf
like a swaying lantern.
My friend watched this scene
and said, "I want to look at this scene,
and memorize it, burn it into my brain,
record it in my mind, so I can call it up when I want to.
So I can have it with me always."

I too have my recorders.
I burn these things into my brain,
I burn these things onto pages.
I pick and choose what needs to be said,
what needs to be remembered.

When I first went to college
I was studying to be a computer science
engineer, I wanted to make a ton of money
I wanted to beat everyone else
because burned in my brain were the taunts
of kids who were in cliques
so others could do the thinking for them
because burned in my brain were the evenings
of the high school dances I never went to

because burned in my brain were the people
I knew I was better than
who thought they were better than me.
Well, yes, I wanted to make a ton of money
I wanted to beat everyone else
but I hated what I was doing
I hated what I saw around me
hated all the pain people put each other through
and all of these memories just kept flooding me
so in my spare time
to keep me sane, to keep me alive
I wrote down the things I could not say
that was how I recorded things.

When I looked around me, and saw friends
raping my friends
I wrote, I burned into these nightmares with a pen
and yes, I have this recorded
I have all of this recorded.

What did you think I was doing
when I was stuffing hand-written notes into my pockets
or typing long hours into the night?
I was sitting in a computer lab
slamming my hands, my fingers against the keyboard
because there were too many atrocities in the world
too many injustices that I had witnessed
too many people who had wronged me —

and I had a lot of work to do.
There had to be a record of what you've done.

Did you think your crimes would go unpunished?
Did you think that I wouldn't remember?
You see, that's what I have my poems for
so there will always be a record
of what you have done.
Yes, I have defiled many pages
in your honor, you who swung your battle ax
and thought no one would remember in the end.
Well, I made a point to remember.
Yes, I have defiled many pages
and have you defiled many women?
You, the man who rapes my friends?
You, the man who rapes my sisters?
You, the man who rapes me?
Is this what makes you a strong man?

you want to know why I do the things I do

I had to record these things
that is what kept me together
when people were dying
that is what kept me together
when my friends went off to war
that is what kept me together
when my friends were raped
and left for dead
that is what kept me together
when no one bothered to notice this
or change this
or care about this
these recordings kept me together

I need to record these things
to remind myself
of where I came from
I need to record these things
to remind myself
that there are things to value
and things to hate
I need to record these things
to remind myself
that there are things worth fighting for
worth dying for
I need to record these things
to remind myself
that I am alive

the Men at the Construction Site

a woman told me
that scientists did an experiment
where a woman
first walked past a construction site
with her head down

no one bothered her,
no one noticed her
everyone at the site left her alone

then, later in the day,
she walked past again
in the same outfit, with the same stride
but this time she walked with
her head up,
more confidently

and that's when she got
the calls, the whistles
from the men at the construction site

and you tell me it's not deliberate
and you tell me it's not an effort
to keep women in their place

God Eyes

It was a stupid point to argue about at 2 a.m.,
sitting in the lobby of the Las Vegas Hilton
listening to the clink and whirr of slot machines
and the dropping of tokens onto metal.
You believed in God, I did not. Even after two
rounds of Sam Adams and three rounds of Bailey's
I knew you wouldn't change my mind, and
I had no desire to change yours.

You told me of a dream you had: in it you and
Christian Slater played a game of pool. You
won. He looked at his hands and said, "I've got
a beer in one hand, and a cigarette in the other.
I guess this means it's time for me to seduce
someone." And he walked away. You're a funny
man. You make me laugh. Your brother even noticed
that. And you even spoke like Slater, rough, mysterious.

You were the optimist: yes, there is
meaning to life. I was doomed to nothingness,
meaninglessness. But to me you were the
pessimist: you believed you were not
capable of creating the power, the passion
you had within you. I had control in my life, even
if in the end it was all for nothing.
You think we are so different. We are not.

It's now after three and we listen to music:
Al Jarreau, Whitney Houston, Billy Ocean, Mariah
Carey. Natalie Cole, with her father. "That's why darling,
it's incredible -" you mouth as you walk toward the
washrooms - "that someone so unforgettable -"
take a spin, watch me mouth the words
with you as you walk away -
"think that I am unforgettable too."

I tell you about the first time I got drunk - I was
maybe ten, and asked my sister to make a mixed
drink mom had that I liked. She made me a few.
So there I was, walking to the neighbor's house in
the summertime, wearing my sister's seventies
zip-up boots, oversized and unzipped, carrying my
seventh drink and sticking my tongue out to see the
grenadine. You liked my story. You laughed.

Passion is a hard thing to describe. Passion
for life. You must know and understand a
spirituality behind it. You do your work, the things
in life solely because you must - it is you,
and you could not exist any other way. It is
who you are. It is a feeling beyond mere
enjoyment. You said that the spirituality was a God.
I said it was my mind. Once again, we lock horns.

All of my life I have seen people espouse beliefs
but not follow them. Tell me you're not like them.
Our values are different, but tell me we both have
values and will fight to the death for them. I need to know
that there are people like that, like me. We are different,
but at the core we are the same. We understand all this.
I'm grasping straws here as the clock says 3:45 a.m.
and the betting odds for football games roll by

on the television screen. You don't gamble. Neither
do I. Why must you be so far away? You reminded
me that I have a passion in life, that I have to
keep fighting. But I get weak and tire
of fighting these battles alone. I, the
atheist, have no God and have to rely on
my will. When I am low, I struggle. You have
your God to fall back on, I only have me.

And you looked into my eyes as it approached
the morning. You stared. We locked horns once
again. I ask you again what you were
thinking. And you said, "I see God in
your eyes." Later you said it to me again. I asked
you what you meant. You said, "I see
a God in your eyes. I see a soul." Whether
what you saw was your God or just me, my

passion, well, thank you for finding it. "Good-bye,
Ms. Kuypers," you said when you left for good
that day. I said nothing. Good-bye, Mr. Williams,
I thought, then I closed the door, walked to the
window, started singing unforgettable. I was alone
in my hotel room, and the lights from the Stardust,
the Frontier, the Riviera were still flashing.
I'm not alone. Good-bye, Mr. Williams.

Being God

I'm tired of dying for your sins
over and over again and why is it that
I am the one that's doing the dying
when you are the one that's doing the sinning
I don't think you're learning your lesson

I'm tired of taking this knife to my hands
over and over again giving myself the stigmata
the blood gets all over my clothes
and I can never get the stains out
and for what, for you to see how I suffer

I'm tired of being humble when I'm
supposed to be the one with the power
over and over again I become your servant
and never are you bowing to me
I don't even get a thank you

I'm tired of preaching to the converted
when the converted aren't even really listening
they're snoring in the back rows while I
deliver my sermon and there's not even air
conditioning in here and I'm sweating

I'm tired of coming to you and healing the sick
taking away the problems, over and over again
giving you something to look forward to
and all I have is an eternity of waiting for
someone to take my place and tend to my wounds

I'm tired of giving the earth up to you
watching the devil's work be done, and you know,
he's just sitting down there looking at me
and laughing, over and over again because it's
so easy for him when he doesn't have to work

I'm tired of being your salvation
over and over again you turn to me
and I have no one to turn to but myself
it's a bitch, you know, being your own god
since no one can save me from me

I'm tired of being your teacher, handing you
what you need on a silver platter and waiting
for that damn collection plate and someone
is always stealing out of it from the back row
I know who you are, you who leave me nothing

I'm tired of wearing this crown of thorns
over and over again the needles prick my skin
and even gods bleed, at least this one does
and when I ask you to wipe the blood
out of my eyes, well, I can't see you anywhere

I'm tired of being something for everybody
when everyone is nothing for me
maybe the devil has the right idea, you know
maybe I'll sit back and wait for you to miss me
as you wonder who's your messiah now

Too Far *(2020 edit)*

When he met me
he told me
I looked like
Gwyneth Paltrow,
Cameron Diaz,
Kim Basinger —
long blonde locks

but as time
wore on I knew
I wasn't her
and I could never
be her   and I was
never good enough
thin enough
pretty enough

so I got a perm
straightened my
teeth
bought a wonder
bra   but it wasn't
doing the trick

I bought SlimFast
used the stair
stepper   ate rice
cakes and wheat
germ but I wasn't
thin enough   I

only dropped
twenty pounds

so I went to the
spa   got my skin
peeled   soaked
myself in mud
wrapped myself
in cellophane
bought the amino
acid facial creams
but I knew they
didn't really
work

so I went to
the doctor   got my
nose slimmed
my tummy stapled
my thighs sucked

thought about
getting a rib or two
removed
you know
like Cher

but I figured
my ribs?
they've got to
be there for
something
and hey, that's
just going
too far

I'm Thinking About Myself Too Much

all of my life it
has all been about you
what do you need
what do you want
how can i help you
what can i do for you
and now for once
i start to live
and now you tell me
that i'm thinking about
myself too much
and i think back to
all the time i've
spent with you
and all the care
i've given you
and now you tell me
that i'm thinking about
myself too much
and i've cooked for
you and i've cleaned
for you and i've made
sure everything in
your world made sense
and now you tell me
that i'm thinking about
myself too much
and all i can think
is that you're only angry
because i'm thinking
about me at all

Why I'll Never Get Married

 at work we've been looking
for a new employee
we've sifted through resumes
we've interviewed a few

and some were good
some were very good
and we took some time to decide
and then we called our #1 choice

and they said they wanted
more money than we offered
so we said our goodbyes
and we called our second choice

and they said they couldn't work
at such a small place
so someone at work said
we should interview some more

and that's when i knew
at the rate we were going
we'd never find anyone
and no one would want us

Barbie

My sister-in-law gave me a Midge doll set
when she married my brother. Midge came complete
with a wardrobe of designer floor-length dresses,
with sequins, and tulle, and three-quarter-length gloves.

But Midge, an older model, had short red hair
styled like a housewife, not like Barbie's, long and
blond and flowing. And Midge could never sit in a chair
because her plastic legs were rigid and couldn't bend.

For my sixth birthday I received a P.J. doll,
one of Barbie's friends. P.J.'s hair was blonde, like
Barbie's, but it was shorter. And here eyes were brown,
like mine. Not eyes to dream of. Eyes like mine.

When I finally got you, Barbie, I treated you like
some sort of goddess, you with your disproportionate
figure and perpetual smile. When you never eat,
you can stay thin. You can always be happy.

I took plastic kitchen shelf liner and caulking glue
and lined a shoebox so you could have a bath tub.
I taped a straw around the back of the tub so you
could have jets and extra bubbles when you soaked.

My father's pool table was your lake; a second
shoe box served as your speed boat. You took all
your friends for boat rides along the green; Ken,
the Donny and Marie dolls, P.J., even Midge.

But I couldn't be like you, I had to eat, and I could only
stand on my toes for so long when you stood like
a dancer perpetually. I couldn't always smile. I was
only a little girl. And I was cursed with brown eyes.

What did you teach me? I pressed you next to Ken
under your pink and white bed sheets, but your plastic
bodies made a loud noise when you came together.
Your legs never intertwined. Your smile never changed.

And now, all grown up, I visit my parent's house,
and they tell me I have boxes of toys that could be
thrown away. Kitchen accessories for the Barbie
camper, beaded dresses I made myself. And I think:

I could give these toys to my niece, so she could play,
so she could learn. And then I decide: no, these dolls,
these values, these memories, they belong sealed
in cardboard boxes, where only time can take its toll.

The One At Mardi Gras

i was at mardi gras last weekend
and i got a bunch of beads from parades
(no, i didn't lift my shirt for them) -

and a friend of mine had a balcony
on bourbon street, and so we were on it
on friday night, and the swarms

of people stretched for over a mile. it was
a mob, no one could walk and the crowd
just kind of carried them along. and all

the men expected women to get naked
for them for beads, and from my balcony
i would see every few minutes a series of

flash pops, coupled with a roar from the
crowd, and i knew a woman lifted her shirt
for the screaming masses. i refused, however,

to strip for drunk strangers, when i knew
they all expected me to, being on a balcony
and all. so men would look up at me and stretch

out their arms, looking up inquisitively, as
if to ask either for me to give them beads
or for me to strip. and since i wasn't stripping

and had plenty of my own beads, i decided
to turn the tables and see if men would accept
the same conditions they asked of these women.

when they looked up at me for something,
i would say, "drop your pants." they would look up
at me, confused, because the women are the

ones that are supposed to be stripping, but
in general i got two responses from the men:
either they would look at me like i was

crazy and walk away, or they would shrug,
as if to say, "okay," and then they would
start unzipping their pants. then they would

make a gesture to turn around, as if to ask,
"do you want to see my butt?" and that's when i'd
yell, "the front," and then they'd turn back

around, with their pants and their underwear
at their knees, and start moving their hips
(which i never asked for, by the way).

so over the course of the evening i
managed to get at least twenty men to
strip like this for me, and i was amazed

that there was this society, this micro-
cosm of society, that allowed this kind
of debauchery in the streets, a sort of

prostitution-for-plastic-beads form of
capitalism. so i was reveling in this bizarre
annual ritual when this man, average to

everyone else, wearing grey and minding
his own business, decided to look up at me. so
i asked him to drop his pants, and instead of

disgustedly leaving or willingly obliging
he crossed both hands on his chest and looked
up at me, as if to ask, "you want to me do

what? you naughty, naughty girl." and he
smiled and looked up at me, and it occurred
to me that i finally found someone in this

massive crowd that thinks they way i do.
now, new orleans has a population, from what i
hear, of about one million, but during mardi gras

there are about nine or ten million people, and
all i could think was that of all these people
here, i finally found someone who wouldn't

blindly do what i asked, but at the same time
wouldn't think i was crazy for asking.
of course as i looked at him i also happened

to think that he was stunning, by far the best-
looking man i had seen that entire night, he
looked like he had style, like he was self-

confident, but then again, i'm near-sighted
and was on a balcony drunk at mardi gras.
we hit an impasse when he wouldn't strip

and neither would i, so his attention was
eventually diverted to other balconies. but i
noticed for that next half-hour that he never left

from under my balcony, and every once in a while
he would still turn around and look up at me. oh,
boy, i was thinking the entire time, i know

this is no way to start a relationship, hell,
i'm sure this guy lives nowhere near me, and
i haven't even had a real conversation with him,

but he's damn near perfect. and all that time we
were screaming and partying at mardi gras,
he would still occasionally turn around and

make sure i was still there. and finally he
looked at me, signaling that he had to move
on with his friends, and i held up my index

finger to make him wait and then i threw
a bunch of beads at him. part of me threw
them because he was a good sport, putting

up with my taunting and still not giving in,
but a part of me threw them because i
saw in him the strong values and the sense

of self-worth, the sheer love of life, the
desire to be alive, that i possessed all along
and have always longed for in someone else.

Who You Tell your Dreams to

we were driving down the freeway
you and me in the pick-up truck
and your girlfriend in between
where you could move the gear shift
and it would mean so much to you

and you saw something that you thought
was beautiful, and you said, "look
at the lines, look at how it was made"
and you were inspired by the beauty
of an everyday object no one else noticed

and your girlfriend, riding in the middle
said "that's him, people think he's crazy"
and i thought, "no, it just depends on who
you tell your dreams to" but i couldn't
say it in the truck i wouldn't say it

You and Me and Your Girlfriend

we went out for drinks together
you and me and your girlfriend
to a restaurant in Malibu
with a balcony that hung over the water

had a perfectly lovely time
you and me and your girlfriend
talking about life, catching up
and you suggested that we go out on the balcony

and I thought that would be charming
for you and me and your girlfriend
but we hadn't paid our bill yet
so your girlfriend told us to go on without her

we stood outside, leaned on the rail
you and me
listened to the water crash on the rocks
below us and we talked

but now it was not about catching up
you and me
it was about ideas, dreams, plans
and before I knew it we were out there

for nearly an hour, and I said,
"what about your girlfriend?"
she was waiting for us all that time
and you said, "oh, yeah" and didn't move an inch

Just By Holding His Hand

when we're walking down the street in stride
and our feet pump out the same rhythm
and our shoulders are almost touching
and our hands seem to brush up against
and along each other for one brief moment

in that one brief moment, our hands almost touch
and he reaches over and takes my hand
he slides his fingers around my hand
and I feel him move along my palm to my fingers

when he moves along my palm to my fingers
no one knows what it feels like then
when his fingers curl and hold me tight
well, it feels like... pop rocks

you know when it feels like pop rocks
that candy is sliding down your throat
after you let it explode on your tongue
and it's tingling, oh, you know that feeling
and no one else is eating these pop rocks
and no one knows that tingling feeling
and this is my little secret

and I love keeping this little secret
when I feel this feeling like never before
and it makes me want to laugh and cry
because when I look around the room
I know no one else is eating those pop rocks
and no one knows the feeling when he's holding my hand

no one knows the feeling when he's holding my hand
it's like candy and cupids and hearts and sunshine
and all those generic symbols of love
that never explain it just right

words can never explain it just right,
it's catching your breath, falling from an airplane
it's climbing a mountain, it's standing on a glacier,
it's following dolphins, it's swimming with sharks
it's turning your head and seeing those fingers
interlocked with yours as you're walking in stride

because then and there, walking in stride
you think of those pop rocks, tingling down your throat
but now this feeling hits all of your nerves
because pop rocks never felt like this

and now nothing has ever felt like this
it's in all of your muscles and all of your nerves
and now you want to hold on for your life
you now feel something you've never felt before
all
        just by holding his hand

The Way You Tease Me

What I think I like the most about you
is the way you always leave me wanting more.
When you kiss me, and we start to pull back
I want to cock my head and kiss you again
but I never know if you'll let me.

What I think I like the most about you
is the way you roll your sultry deep voice over me
like a wave of heat on a summer afternoon.
You use a pause to tease me with your words
until sweat dances down my hairline and tickles me neck.

What I think I like the most about you
is the way you slide your arms around my waist
and make me just want to collapse in your grasp
and run my hands up and down your back
until I hear you moan and sigh.

What I think I like the most about you
is the way that absence makes the heart grow fonder
and when we touch you say we should take it slow,
take our time, enjoy every moment
and you know, you couldn't be more right.

What I think I like the most about you
are the things that make me think I have to fight for you
are the things that make me second guess myself
because nothing's ever easy, not you, not me,
not relationships, not sex, not love.

What I think I like the most about you
is the wondering, is the waiting, is the teasing.
That's what I like. This high-charged guessing game.
The flirting. The first touch. The first everything.
Thinking about the possibilities. Yeah. That's what I like.

There I Sit

there I sit

I sit alone
separated
isolated
away from my only love
my obsession

I pull out
a fountain pen
I look
at the lines
the contours
of his face

defining
the piercing
eyes
the pointed
nose
the tender
lips

I feverishly
draw
I sketch
I capture
his image

I stare
I gaze
I memorize his every detail
but he never looks back

so I will draw
until my
fountain pen
runs dry

And I'm Wondering

I'm wondering if there's something
chemical that brings people together,
something that brings people to their
knees, somethings that sucks them in

And I'm wondering if you're sensing what I'm
sensing, is it just me, am I making this up
in my head, or when I glance up and catch your
eyes, well, are you actually staring at me

And I'm wondering if it could work out this
time, if we'd have one of those relationships
that no one ever doubts, especially us,
because we know we'll always be in love

And I'm wondering if you'd find
my neurotic pet-peeves charming
like how I hate it when someone touches
my belly because I'm so self conscious

And I'm wondering why you had to tell me
when we happened to be sitting next to each
other that the fact that our legs were almost
touching was making your heart race

And I'm wondering why I felt the need
to take your cigarette and inhale, exhale
while the filter was still warm from
your lips, there just seconds before

And I'm wondering if a year or two from now,
after we've been going out and should have
gotten to the point where we are bored with
each other and sink into a comfortable rut

if you saw me making macaroni and cheese
in the kitchen using margarine and water
because I'm out of milk and I've got my hair
pulled back and strands are falling into my

eyes and I'm wearing an oversized button-down
denim shirt and nothing else, well, what
I'm wondering is if you would see me
like this and still think I was sexy

When I glance up and catch your eyes from
across the room, when I see your eyes dart
away, when I feel this chemical reaction, well,
it makes me wonder if you can feel it too

Looking for a Worthy Adversary
(an extreme sestina variation)

I've been looking for a worthy adversary
someone I can lock horns with —
though my life makes more sense when I'm alone
it's not nearly as interesting

alone, it's not nearly as intreesting,
so I look for a worthy adversary
someone I can battle to the death with
because it can't be about love, you see
love can't exist on the terms I demand
it's never that pure

what I demand is never that purse,
as I'm looking for a worthy adversary
I slither up to you like a snake
and I tempt you with a golden apple

I tempt you with that golden apple
but all I'm offering you
is fruit from the tree of knowledge

this snake gives you the tree of knowledge
because all this time I've been playing a part
an actress on stage, spouting lines on cue
but that role was tiresome,
those lights came on night after night
and I still had to play my part

I played my part
until my night off, where I saw your show
your protagonist was doing what I was doing
right down to faking it with those who don't matter
right down to going home and still feeling empty

I play my part, I still feel empty
but I liked to see your boiling emotion underneath
no one else could see

I know what that emotion really means

when I know what that emotion really means
I wonder if we can get together
and write our own play

if we wrote our own play,
it would be a masterful performance
curtains would close,
we'd hold each other's hands
as we leave the stage
and the audience would know there's a happy ending

when I know there's a happy ending
I walk out on to the set
and there you stand, in front, stage left
I wait for my cue to make my move
none of the rest of the scene matters

if the rest of the scene doesn't really matter,
I wonder if the audience would see what we have...
maybe they'd like our little play,
maybe they wouldn't
who really cares

who really cares
because after I tempted you
you now tempt me and tease me and torment me
and tell me everything I was afraid to believe

I was afraid to believe
and now you talk,
you reach your hand into my brain
and pull out my thoughts
and shove them into your mouth
and spit them back at me

you spit my thoughts back at me again
and instead of filling me with terror
it fills me with joy

it fills me with joy
because I thought I'd lock horns
with that worthy adversary —
but now every day is like Valentine's Day,
it's like candy and flowers and springtime
and hearts and cupids and sunshine

and these clichés are beginning to make sense

no longer locking horns,
and everything making sense,
I stand here like a statue
after the performance of our lifetime
and wait for the reviews

as I wait for the reviews
I wonder what they'll say
though none of it matters

none of it matters
because I know what you are going to say
it's everything that I've always wanted to say

all I ever wanted to say
is now you, taking my thoughts again
and shoving them into your mouth again
and spitting them back at me again
so I will wait for you to come on stage again
where we have our happy ending
and you tell me what I already know

Us, Actually Touching

I heard a physicist explain
that when two solid objects
are pressed together
they never actually touch

I can't imagine it
but maybe
because electrons repel
all objects remain one molecule apart

I wonder if this is why
when I see you
and when we embrace
I want to hold you tighter and tighter

because I want to defy
the laws of physics
and feel that contact with you
as long as I possibly can

is this why whenever we embrace
I want my face at your neck
so that I inhale you deeply
I breathe you in

because I want to experience you
with all my senses
I want our molecules to intermingle
I want us to actually touch

run faster

why me
why do I keep doing this to myself
why do I keep coming back

I beg for attention
and I don't know how to stop
and I don't know how to be alone

so I keep giving you
one more chance to make it perfect
one more chance to save the damsel

but I'm not a damsel
and I'm not being rescued
and I'm not feeling any better

because even though I hate you
I'll never let go
so you'll just have to run faster

All These Reminders

Look, over here, in my living room.
You left an empty bottle of beer
on the end table. The cap, too.
And come here, follow me, over here,
in the kitchen, look in here, see,
you left some of your food in the pantry.
A box of spaghetti, some canned
tomatoes. And come here, in the bathroom,
I know you probably won't notice this,
but here, this towel, it smells like
you, is smells like your shaving cream.
And I could swear my crumpled bed
sheets are still warm from you.

Why did you have to go. Why
does this have to seem so hard.

Okay, look here, the remote for the
television is on the arm of the chair,
where you always leave it. And the cocktail
table, it's pushed forward on one side
because you'd always rest your feet
on it. Everywhere I look around me,
I see something that you affected.
I look in the kitchen. I look in the
dining room. I look in the mirror.

Why did you do this to me. Why
couldn't you have made a clean break.

There's still some of your messages
scribbled on scraps of paper next to
the phone in the kitchen. And look,
the pillow on the couch is bunched
up because you could never get
comfortable with it. And over here,
the phone books are out on the
kitchen counter, you never put them
away, and here they are, still sitting
out, I'll have to put them back in the
cabinet. and look here, why do I
still have all of your love letters
stuffed into a drawer in my desk.

When you left me, why did you
have to leave me all these reminders.

Protecting Peace can Put you in Prison

The first Nobel Peace Prize was granted in 1901.
The first Nobel Peace laureate to die in prison
was Carl von Ossietzky, detained by Nazi Germany;
he died in prison in 1938. But there's a new death,
do not fret, because is seems that peace can be
squashed in any millennia.

Do you remember
the Tiananmen Square Riots back in 1989? Or at least
the iconic photo of a student in front of a tank?
Well, the students didn't battle the Chinese government
on their own and win, they had help from Liu Xiaobo.
This man for peace was revered for his work,
but the Chinese government stopped him in 2008,
because he was drafting and promoting a manifesto
promoting peaceful political change. And for this,
the Chinese government imprisoned him for "subversion".

Yes, for "subversion", this man was sentenced
to eleven years in prison, and it was while in prison
that he was granted the Nobel Peace Prize.

During that Oslo awards ceremony, they left
an empty chair for their imprisoned man of honor.

And now the Chinese government bears responsibility,
more than for imprisoning a Nobel Peace laureate
who only promoted peaceful politics, but for
failure to properly diagnose and treat his ailments,

because on 7/13 the imprisoned Peace Prize
winner died in detention of liver cancer at age 61.

\#

And sure, we can look around the room and think
that we are nice to other people, that we respect
other people. And we may think as we look around
that other people feel the same way toward us.

And it's wonderful to surround yourself with people
like you, who think like you, who cushion you
from anyone who may think differently. Because
when you stay in your bubble, everything seems fine.

But it's only when we see those who choose to fight,
those who are trounced upon and downtrodden
only because they support a peaceful coexistence,
that staying with supporters is seldom the solution.

Peace with the ones you choose to know is one thing.
Peace with a mortal enemy is another, when others
decide you are at fault for some unknown reason.
So maybe the key to promoting peace

is not to share our ideas with those like-minded souls
you're near, but to find the people least like you,
religiously, racially, politically, and just extend your hand.
In peace. And *then* see who will take your hand.

Effigy

When it gets hot like this, when the summer drags on,
then is when you wonder when heat and pain will end.
It's as if a fire has been set to the entire land, and this
fire is within the hearts of men still set out to do you in.

Low winds come across the plains, rustling leaves and
anything hanging from the trees. And after this heat
that you've suffered through for far too long, all you can
see are your brothers hanging from those trees in effigy.

Then when we fight, we even use your rules, and still
you will do everything in your power to stop us from
having the rights we have always deserved. It may take
years for us to come together to truly try to make real

chance, but even when we agree we should all be free,
the blockades we think are forever down will still remain.
We want to be free, and we will always fight. But we will
always feel the flames on our backs, as we face the wind.

This poem was written 8/28, the day in 1955 black teenager Emmett Till was
brutally murdered in a lynching, galvanizing the civil rights movement; the day in
1957 where U.S. Senator Strom Thurmond filibustered to prevent voting on the
Civil Rights Act; and the day in 1963 of the March on Washington for Jobs and
Freedom and Reverend Martin Luther King, Jr.'s "I Have a Dream" speech.

more than we should have

when i think of him i usually think about the drinking

actually, i never think of him as drinking
come to think of it
i just think of him as drunk
i can't even remember seeing the drinks in his hand
but his perception of the world is always altered

but someone reminded me tonight
of when he would work outside in the the cold Chicago winters
and he would come back with his moustache frozen
and there would be little icicles hanging
down toward his mouth

and then i thought of
when i waited with him once at the airport
because we were picking up someone
and we sat in the shrimp cocktail lounge
and he drank, and ate, and i waited

and as we left
we tried to pay the expressway toll with pennies
but some of the coins fell onto the street
and we had to throw more change at the machine

we paid more than we should have
i'm sure we did

The Truth Is Out There

We were of the same clan.
We were of the same kin.
We were brothers —
yes, we were compatriots,
underlyingly, inextricably
bound together.

We're supposed to be
so close, so I should know
what happened inside you.
I need to understand
what changed you so deeply,
how you lost your humanity.

I've scoured the world
to try to learn
what happened to you.
We all noticed the change,
that your sense of the world
was always altered

even though we seldom
remember a drink in your hand.
The truth is out there,
is what I hear, but
is that the key to unlocking
how you relate to me.

Is the truth not out there,
but deep inside you instead,
or do you not see the change
that has happened to your soul,
do you not see
the changes under your skin.

Something has infected you,
or maybe you let it in
and it destroyed your business,
your marriage, and any love
you may have ever felt
from your only daughter.

I don't know if I can
find the answers to unlock
the now inhuman part of you.
They say the truth is out there,
if only I knew where to look,
and only if you'd want to be found.

The State of the Nation *(2016 edit)*

my phone rang earlier today
and I picked it up and said "hello"
and a man on the other end said,
Is this Janet Kuypers?
and I said, "Yes, it is, may I ask
who is calling?"
and he said, Yeah, hi, this is
George Washington, and I'm sitting here
with Jefferson and a couple
other guys here and we wanted to
tell you a few things. And I said
"Why me?" And he said Excuse me,
I believe I said I was the one
that wanted to do the talking.
God, that's the problem with
Americans nowadays. They're so
damn rude. And I said, "You know,
you really didn't have to use
language like that," and he said,
Oh, I'm sorry, it's just I've been
dead so long, I lose all control
of my manners. Well, anyway, we just
wanted to tell you some stuff. Now,
you know that we really didn't have
much of an idea of what we were
doing when we were starting up
this country here, we didn't have
much experience in creating
bodies of power, so I could understand
how our Constitution could be
misconstrued

and then he put in a dramatic pause
and said,
but when we said people had
a right to bear arms
we meant to protect themselves
from a government gone wrong
and not so you could kill
a sixteen year old girl
at an A.T.M. at six P.M.
for twenty dollars cash
and when we said freedom of
religion we included the separation
of church and state because freedom
of religion could also mean freedom
from religion
and when we said freedom of speech
we had no idea you'd be
burning a flag
or painting pictures of Christ
doused in urine
or photographing people with
whips up their respective anatomies
but hell, I guess we've got to
grin and bear it
because if we ban that
the next thing they'll ban is books
and we can't have that
and I said, "But there are schools
that have books banned, George."
And he said Oh.

Andrew Hettinger

I never really liked you. You never revealed
yourself to me and why would you: you,
who never had anyone, you, who always
had the bad breaks. Everyone looked at you
as different. Where would you have learned
to trust. Who would you have learned it from.

I never really liked you. I met you through
a friend and he explained to me that multiple
sclerosis left you with a slight limp and a
faint lisp. Faint, under the surface, but there,
traces of something no one would ever
know of you well enough to fully understand.

I never really liked you. You never revealed
yourself to me and I never wanted you to;
you scared me too much. You, plagued with
physical ailments. You, with a limp in your walk.
You, with a patch over your eye. You, who
stared at me for always just a bit too long.

They told me the patch was from eye surgery
with complications and now you had to cover
your shame, cover someone else's mistakes,
cover a wrong you didn't commit, cover a
problem not of your own doing. The problems
were never of your own doing, were they.

I heard these stories and I thought it was sad.
I heard these stories and thought you had to be

a pillar of strength. And then I saw you drink,
straight from the bottle, fifteen-year-old
chianti. And I saw you smash your hand into
your living room wall. This is how you lived.

The house you lived in was littered with
trash. Why bother to clean it up anyway. It
detracted you from the holes in the wall, the
broken furniture from drunken fits. This was
how you reacted to life, to the world. You didn't
know any better. This is how you coped.

I never really liked you. You would come home
from work, tell us about a woman who was
beautiful and smart that liked you, but she
wasn't quite smart enough. And I thought: We
believe anything if we tell ourselves enough.
We weave these fantasies to get through the days.

I never really liked you. Every time you talked
to me you always leaned a little too close. So
I stayed away from the house, noted that those
whom you called friends did the same. I asked
my friend why he bothered to stay in touch.
And he said to me, "But he has no friends."

This is how I thought of you. A man who was
dealt a bad hand. A man who couldn't fight
the demons that were handed to him. And
with that I put you out of my mind, relegated
you to the ranks of the inconsequential. We parted
ways. You were reduced to a sliver of my youth.

I received a letter recently, a letter from
someone who knew you, someone who wanted
me to tell my friend that they read in the
newspaper that you hanged yourself. Your
brother died in an electrical accident, and
after the funeral you went to the train

station; instead of leaving this town you
went to a small room and left us forever.
Strangers had to find you. The police had to
search through records to identify your body.
The newspaper described you as having "health
problems." But you knew it was more than that.

And I was asked to be the messenger to my
friend. The funeral had already passed. You were
already in the ground. There was no way he
could say goodbye. I shouldn't have been the one
to tell him this. No one deserved to tell him.
He was the only one who tried to care.

I never really liked you. No one did. But when
I had to tell my friend, I knew his pain.
I knew he wanted to be better. I knew he
thought you were too young to die. I knew he
felt guilty for not calling you. He knew it
shouldn't have been this way. We all knew it.

I never really liked you. But now I can't get
you out of my mind; you haunt me for all the
people we've forgotten in our lives. I don't like
what you've done. I don't like you quitting.
I don't like you dying, not giving us the chance
to love you, or hate you, or even ignore you more.

My friend still doesn't know where your grave is.
I'd like to find it for him, and take him to you.
Let you know you did have a friend out there.
Bring you a drink, maybe, a fitting nightcap
to mark your departure, to commemorate a life
filled with liquor, violence, pain and death.

I never really liked you, but maybe we could get
together in some old cemetery, sit on your grave
stone, share a drink with the dead, laugh at the
injustices of life when we're surrounded by death.
Maybe then we'd understand your pain for one brief
moment, and remember the moments we'll always regret.

Walking Home from School

once when I was little

I was walking home from school
filled with fear, like I always was

the other kids made fun of me
they called me names
sometimes they threw rocks at me
once they pushed me to the ground
went home, bleeding knees and tears

but once, I'll never forget, Patti
from 121st street was
walking behind me and threw
her gym shoes at me

they landed right next to me
as I was walking down
that first big hill

I don't know if I stopped
but I remember for a brief moment
looking up at the tall tree branches
next to the road

all the entangled dead branches

and I thought
that all I had to do

was pick up her shoes
and throw them

as hard as I could

and she would never
get her shoes back

I looked at the trees
for only a moment
and I continued walking
as fast as I could
as I always did
and suddenly the shoes
were long behind me

and the others were laughing

I look back now
and wonder why I didn't
do it

was I scared of them
was I scared of myself

I still keep asking myself that

Made Any Difference

So I'm at my bar
my favorite hang-out
I just overheard
from people talking

that another guy
who's always here
in the past few months
has had a few strokes

now, this is grapevine
I just heard snippets
but I needed to see him
put in my two cents

he went out for a smoke
and even though I don't
I walked up to him
after he lit up

I reached my hand out
toward his cigarette
he offered me a new one
but... I wanted his

then holding his smoke
I told him I heard
I talked about his wife
asked about his kids

and I don't want to
get on a high horse here
but we care for him
we want him happy

he said I was right
he'll take some time off
then holding his smoke
said that he should quit

he handed me his smoke
and then walked away

I stood there a while
sucking nicotine
wondering if I
made any difference

One by One, the Beech Trees Fell

i have lived at this grove all my life
the beautiful trees have always lined the roads
the beech trees even lined the drive to our home

everything was blooming by the end of May
when you came in from the coast to our home
and the war didn't touch here

could hear noise in the distance one morning
he told me some trees have been already been felled
on the General Field Marshall's urgent orders

Rommel was sure an attack was immanent
they couldn't leave trees for enemy hideouts
and so they fell our trees, one by one

looked out the front door, saw our stripped land
these trees had souls, and no one mourns
the loss of a species with roots in this land longer than we

they didn't do this everywhere:
i hear they left some trees up in fields
so glider planes would be destroyed while landing

what lives are worth saving, i thought
as the soldiers continued doing their job
after the beech trees fell

Unmarried Women
and Dead Bodies Everywhere

the Ganges River in India,
the most sacred river to Hindus
is still religiously renowned

but on one day not too long ago,
at one tributary of the Ganges river
they discovered twenty-eight bodies

the locals first spotted the corpses
when vultures surrounded those bodies
as they piled up along the shore

online news sources explain
that bodies may have been left there
when families couldn't afford a burial

and at those same online news sources,
lucky you, you can see videos of dogs
eating at the flesh of the dead

——

but I was there, I read those newspapers
as the *Star of India* came to me daily,
while locals discovered more bodies:

before they found one hundred and four
the local papers explained
that this 'tradition' of "jalpravah"

is a custom in some cultures —

when unmarried women die
their bodies are dumped in the river

—

unrecognizably decomposed,
more and more bodies
of unmarried women

kept floating to the surface
in just a few days,
in the sacred Ganges river

—

I kept looking for an explanation,
and all I could think was that
this river was supposed to be sacred

and I wondered if this is their effort
to give these women a family
in the afterlife, putting them in a river

they call sacred

because I know how they view women
in India, cover their skin, they don't talk back,
because even though women

are treated like nothing by men there,
they'd be less than nothing
if they're not married

Lambs to Heaven's Gate

They tell you the meek shall inherit the earth.
Then they lead their lambs to the slaughter
as I do, to the ones who will follow.
You see, the meek wouldn't know what to do
with their inheritance. They know nothing
of property, ownership, power. I teach them
not to understand these values but to fear them.
To sacrifice. To stay meek. I'm the one
who tells them how to dress, how to walk,
how to kill themselves. All they need is a reason
as long as they don't have to think it through.

People will believe anything if you
tell it to them the right way. Give them a few
tokens and they'll create icons out of you.
But not everyone can guide, can lead the lost.
Give themselves to the followers who need them,
with nothing in return. Like the stars,
which seem so small, so meek from here
yet are unfathomable, uncontrollable.
Like the shepherd, quietly guiding his flock
but holding a stick all the while. I'm the one
who guides them, who guides them to their destiny.

Smelling Sulfur on Nine One One

I'm a journalist.
I can remember
the sounds of the newsroom
as I finished my articles
at one of the computers.
I can still hear
the sounds of the bustling,
of the rushing toward a deadline.

The shuffling of papers
was a constant presence
when you worked.

Hearing that low hum,
that din of action and activity
is almost comforting
to types like us.
It was the base beat
to the symphony of our lives.

So, when you hear the words
nine one one,
you think of the number to dial
when you hear of more gun violence
on these Chicago streets.
You smell the Sulfur
in the gunpowder,
another sense
that accentuates the center
of the world around us...

But on a beautifully
sunny day like today,
you come into the newsroom
in the early morning,
and the sound of action
has yet to truly penetrate the ears
of these reporters,
with a Styrofoam coffee cup in one hand,
crumpled pages of edited copy in the other.

But on this sunny morning,
the din was different,
much more cacophonous,
much more rushed,
while still so hushed.
I made my way
to one of the TV sets
along the main wall,
all were on different channels
showing different bits of news,
though all suddenly seemed the same.
It looked like the newsroom
was watching a movie
as smoke poured
from one of the Twin Towers.
I tried to make out the voices
from one of the TV sets
when I witnessed a plane —
right before my eyes —
fly into the other Tower.

I stood for a moment,
transfixed like some

horror movie addict,
before I thought of our contacts
scattered along the east coast.
I pulled out my cell phone
and speed dialed Mark in New York,
he had a meeting scheduled
in the Twin Towers that morning,
but the phone was jammed,
so I dialed up Don
who was in town there this week,
but all was lost
to computer-simulated voices,
forcing me to leave messages
and scramble from afar.

As pathetic as we were,
we stared at TVs
as most forms of communication
were cut off for us.
Was this an attack on New York,
we struggled to discover
until less than forty minutes later
we saw the two-second long film
replayed repeatedly
from a D.C. security camera
that caught a collision course
crashing of a plane
through the outer rings
of the Pentagon.

Well.
Now the story has changed.

Try to get through
to Dan in D.C.,
was he in the Pentagon today.
The phones still cut me off.
So we scrambled for any data,
looking for a Chicago connection:
the Sears Tower,
the John Hancock building,
these are national icons
that may be under attack...
But before we could gain our bearings,
only twenty-five minutes passed
before a plane crashed
into the ground
near Shanksville, Pennsylvania.

Shanksville, I thought,
I know someone there,
I searched, and found
Anna's number,
but who was I kidding.
Those lines were cut off too.

#

It's a strange feeling,
being a reporter
and not being able
to contact a single person.
Being detached from any lead,
coupled with a sinking feeling,
wondering if any
of the people you know

are physically hurt,
or even alive.

As a journalist,
you really feel hopeless,
like your hands are tied
behind your back.

We give the news.
We're not supposed
to feel so stranded.

#

An hour after
the Pentagon was attacked,
the Sears Tower was evacuated.
This wasn't my beat;
I had no contacts, no one
to help me through this disaster,
so I waited there
in case others
needed any assistance.

I sat back for a moment,
left there to wait,
thinking about
Mark and Don in New York,
Dan in D.C.,
even poor Anna —
I'm sure she's not hurt,
but they're now cut off to me.
As I said,

all I could do
was wait.

Clear your head of the people,
I could hear myself
say to myself.
You're a reporter,
just break down the details
of what you see
instead of thinking of this
as another one of your
human interest articles...

The jet fuel,
the drywall,
all that paper
in those offices,
those people,
trapped,
they're all
hydrogen, carbon, oxygen.
But wait a minute,
in Chicago I think
of the Sulfur smell
when it comes to gunfire.
But jet fuel is Sulfur-laden,
that burning drywall
emits Sulfur gas,
Sulfur's even the third most common
mineral in the human body.

I mean,
I'm a newspaper reporter.

I know that Sulfur-based compounds
are used in pulp
and paper industries.

\#

Yeah, I'm a newspaper reporter.
Just take a breath
and turn your head to the stats.

To clear my head
of the humanity,
the thought of so much Sulfur
being so much a part
of so many details in our lives,
made me think
of the destruction
that Sulfur was so much
a part of today.
I know I stayed here
to give a helping hand,
but with all that Sulfur
on my mind,
suddenly
all I could smell
was the burning,
and I couldn't stop coughing
while I tried to catch my breath.

Tin

If I only had a brain

if I only had a brain

I'd get out from under
this bent tin roof
that covers me
as I sleep at night

tin metal sheets
keep the rain away
but the wind

but the wind

if I only had a brain

I wouldn't use
my old tin cup
to stand and face east
at Canal and Randolph
and ask for change

I wait for commuters
to cross the Chicago river
to get to their train

you see, I wait
at the other side

and the ones with the money
have to walk right by

that's when I rattle
my old tin cup
give them doe eyes
say "God bless"

but if I only had a brain
I wouldn't rattle
my tin cup
and ask for tin change
I'd get myself up

if I only had a brain

I'd have a lot of money
I'd eat at fancy restaurants
I'd wear the plastic bib

if I only had a brain
I wouldn't be poor
drinking
tin cans of Fanta
eating
soup from a tin can
living
on Tin pan alley

if I only had a brain

you might bend me
but I just won't break
'cause if I had a brain
then I'd be great

Beauty in the Eyes of Einstein

I heard NASA scientists say
that Einstein dismissed some of his theories

even some theories we may know all too well

but Einstein didn't like some of his theories
because he thought they weren't beautiful

and I wonder:
what is beauty

is it the geomagnetic abberations
of the Aurora Borealis
dancing along the horizon
at the arctic circle

is it the way you look at me
with those gorgeous doe eyes
after we've been apart so long

is it the scattered collisions from comet
Shoemaker Levy-9 into the planet Jupiter

is it what I feel
when your arms are finally around me
and I don't want to open my eyes
and I never want to let go

is it the eternally changing
whisps of volcanic trails
in the Saturn moon Titan's atmosphere

is it the way that listening
to the music you make
fills me with such energy

or is it converting matter into pure energy
with just the right formula

Einstein believed
"The most beautiful thing
we can experience
is the mysterious.
It is the source
of all art and science."

so am I driven
to look up at the stars in the night sky
to see stars from billions of years ago
to fall in love every night

Einstein reminds us,
"We are all ruled
in what we do
by impulses"

so is it how on impulse
I move a bit closer to you
so I can feel the heat from your body
so close to mine

we ask, what is beauty

they say beauty is in the eye of the beholder
so it makes me wonder

ways to spend your money

I spent a week in Los Angeles recently
visited Beverly Hills, Hollywood, Brentwood
I saw the Hollywood sign
and Marilyn Monroe's hand print in concrete
took my picture with Tom Jones' star

but the one thing I noticed
was that among the shops
that lined the streets of every neighborhood
there were quite a few pet spas
"pet spas," i thought, "pet spas"

Death takes many forms.

It is winter now.
The trees have lost their leaves;
the city is covered in a thin layer of soot and snow.
The grass is dead.
In the sunless sky black birds circle overhead
searching for prey.
An eerie cold settles over everything.
Nothing is growing anymore.

Death takes many forms.
For you, death first came when you were five years old
and your mother had to give you three shots of insulin a day
until you could take a needle to yourself.
Did it hurt to push that needle into your arm, the first time?
Or did it hurt you more to know you had no choice?

Death takes many forms.
Death can be someone telling you without trying
that they are losing their sight.
Behind coke-bottle glasses you would see me and say,
"That's a nice black suit you're wearing."
And I would tell you, "It's green."
And you wouldn't believe me.
You wouldn't hear the howling wind of the changing seasons.

Death takes many forms.
I know what follows the autumn wind.
It is winter now.
Do you remember when it happened?

The changes are subtle, the temperature drops,
first only slightly. It's almost imperceptible.
Only when the first snow falls do you realize
where the seasons have gone.

Death takes many forms.
Death can be a sweat-soaked shirt, the shakes, dizziness
when you needed food.
You would look as pale as a ghost
as I would hold your cold wet arm and steady you.
Quick, some sugar will make everything better.
Isn't everything better yet?

Death takes many forms.
The signs of death can come
when you lose your circulation.
"My feet are numb, Janet," you'd say.
"I can't feel my feet anymore."
And I would rub your feet for you,
and you would say it makes a difference,
you feel better.

If only I could do this forever.

Death takes many forms.
I said good bye to you to travel my own road
but I didn't think it was the last good bye.
How was I to know?

When I left, I knew you didn't want me to go.
And now it's my turn.

Why are we always saying good bye to each other?

Are you trying to teach me a lesson?
Because if you are, well,
I've learned it. Trust me, I have.
You can come back now.

Death takes many forms.
And now, now it seems
you've taken me down with you
you've taken me into that casket with you
and I'm running my hand along your jacket lapel
and I can feel the coldness of winter all around me
and I can hear them shoveling the dirt over my head
and I want to get out
and I want to take you with me.

Death takes many forms.
Death can be that hole you left,
you know, right over here, just a little to the left.
I keep wondering when the pain will go away.
When will everything be better.

You once showed me that winter could be beautiful.
Instead of the dark and dirty snow lacing the city streets
you showed me a quieting snowfall,
over a lake at your parent's back yard
glistening in an untouched whiteness.
I told you I hated winters
and you told me, "This you don't hate."

Well, I'm still learning.

It is winter now.
And death takes many forms.
The seasons change for you and I.
It is snowing. And something is ending.
It is snowing. Somewhere
it is snowing.

Eyes are Blurred to the Battlefield

On the Indonesian island Jawa
large turtle skeletons
litter the plains,

because after they come in
from the ocean
to lay their eggs,

swarms of wild dogs there
all got together
and pounced.

Those wild dogs flip the turtles over,
and strip them all
from their shells

before they eat them alive.

So if you go to the plains on Jawa,
you'll see what looks like
skeletal remains —

and if your eyes are blurred,
you'll swear you're seeing
a battlefield.

Because we cannot forget
that life is a constant
avoidance of death:

because many of those wild dogs
who killed the turtles
are prey to the tiger,

who later pounses up on them.
This is the cycle of life,
because every birth

is a prelude to death.
Remember this.
Don't forget.

When people are young, they're sure
they're invincible, only because
the beat the odds.

But everyone gambles, we call it life,
but you have to remember,
the house always wins.

Everybody thinks they're ahead,
and they forget to
cut their losses —

because most of the time, even if
someone's lived a long life,
are they still happy?

Really?

Death is a Dog

Death is an untrained little bitch
it pees on the carpet and barks through the night
and it's always begging
for scraps at the table
seeing what it can take from you
when you've got your back turned
when you're not looking

when you want it to heal,
well, it never does
and it never rolls over
and it never plays dead

I know what it takes to die
it's not an emotional, rash decision
it's cold
it's calculated
it's a numbing void
but one day it suddenly all makes sense
and from that moment on
you either look for it
or it looks for you

Death is an untrained little bitch
and I've been begging for it, I tell you
but it doesn't come when you call

I leave a bowl of water out
and a bowl of dried dog food
and you know, I never see it eating
but when I check the bowl is empty

and I still refill the bowl

and vacuum the dog hair
that sticks to the couch
and spray air freshener
in the living room
because no matter how hard you try
you can never get rid of the smell

Death is an untrained little bitch, I tell you
and what it boils down to is this:
you won't get along with her
and she won't get along with you

she'll claim her territory
under the bed,
eating your slipper,
while you try to sleep
and remind yourself
that there are no monsters
waiting for you
to shut your eyes

One Summer Traveled

I know we had our differences,
but I was looking forward to seeing you,
to seeing southern California, the stores,
the glamour, the beaches, the commercialism.
And you, you had to cart me away
with your religious troops to the wilderness,
leaving me at a campsite while you went off
to church. And I sat there for days,
watching us, watching us become bloodthirsty,
we were trying to hurt each other, we were like
animals, you starting your life with me in tow.

But at least I saw the redwood forests.

#

And traveling later, I never imagined how beautiful
the east coast could be, rolling hills curling one state
into another. We'd drive up a hill in the truck
and I would lift my head, my chin as high as I could
in anticipation to try to see the other side.
I remember walking along the beach
in Maine, restored buildings lining
the rocky shore, the fog so thick
you couldn't see fifty feet in front of you.
And people were suntanning.

And I photographed the lighthouse -
how do they work in the fog like this?
It's so thick, thick like the cigarette smoke
coming from the inside of the truck
when we would drive to antique shops
in New Hampshire. Thick, like a powerful force
overcoming someone, that
holds you there, that doesn't let go. Like us.

#

Watching this summer, this scenery travel past me
streamline into blurred lines of color,
I think of marriage. Probably not with you,
I just think of marriage, to someone. Marriage,
streamlining life into a blur. Settling down.
Settling. It's funny how your surroundings
can change you.

My Kind of Town

After walking through
the Forbidden City
in Beijing, China
    (where all the palace doorways
    had gold-covered risers
    blocking people's way into rooms
    4 inches to a foot tall,
    because the higher
    your level of authority
    or royalty status
    in the kingdom,
    the higher the bar
    people had to step over —
    not *on,* but over —
    to get inside
    the royalty's room)...
But after the Forbidden City
I entered the Summer Palace.
An old Chinese man
walked up to me
with what I believe was his grand-daughter
walking one foot behind
    though who knows,
    in China
    this one young girl
    could be one
    of his concubines,
    but it's really
    not for me to judge).

But this older Chinese gentleman
walked up and asked,
in the best English he could muster,
where I was from.
So I told him the United States,
and then I said Chicago.
That's when this man's eyes lit up,
and he said,
"My kind of town!"
And I laughed,
nodding my head in agreement
until he leaned in toward me and said,
"Frank Sinatra sang that."
And I laughed again,
"Yes, he did," I said,
because even though
this world is so vast,
we will always find ways
to connect with one another.

Communication *(2020 edit)*

I

now that we have the information superhighway
we can throw out into the open
our screams
our cries for help
so much faster than we could before

our pleas become computer blips
tiny bits of energy
travelling through razor thin wires
travelling through space

to be left for someone to decipher
when they find the time

II

got into work the other day
and got my messages out of voice mail:
mike left me his pager number
and told me to contact him with some information
another mike told me to call him at the office
between ten thirty and noon
lori told me to check my email
because she sent me a message i had to read

so i first returned mike's phone call
but he wasn't in, so i left a message with a coworker

and then i dialed the number for the other mike
listened to an electronic message,
dialed in my own phone number
then i got online, checked my email
read a note from ben, emptied out the junk mail

realizing i didn't actually get a hold of anybody
i tried to call my friend sheri
but i got her answering machine
so i said,
"hi - it's me, janet -
haven't talked to you in a while - "
at which point i realized
there was nothing left to say -
"so,
give me a call, we should really
get together and talk"

III

sara and i were late for carol's wedding rehearsal
which was a bad thing, because we were both
standing up in the wedding
and we were stuck in traffic, and i asked,
"sara, you have a cel phone, don't you?"
and she said "yes"
and i asked, "well, do you know carol's
cel phone number, cause if you do, we can
call her and tell her we'll be late -"
and she said, "no - do you know it?"
and i said "no"

IV

I was out at a bar with Dave, and I was explaining to him
why I hadn't talked to my friend Aaron in a while:
"You see, we usually email each other,
and when we do, we just hit 'reply.'
when you get an email from someone,
instead of having to start a new letter
and get their email address, you can
just hit the 'reply' button on the email message,
and it will make a letter addressed
to the person who wrote you the letter originally.
so one of us sent the other a letter, and
it had a question at the end,
so i hit 'reply' and sent a response,
with another question at the end of my letter.
so we kept having to answer questions for each other,
and we just kept replying to each other,
sending a letter with the same title back and
forth to each other. well, once i got an email
from him and there was no question at the end,
and so i didn't have to send him a response.
so i didn't. and we never thought
to start a new email to one another.
so we just lost touch."

and then it occurred to me, how difficult it had become
to type an extra line of text, because that's why
i lost touch with him

and then it occurred to me, no matter how many different
forms of communication we have,
we'll still find a way
to lose touch with each other

V

now that we have the information superhighway
we can throw out into the open
our screams
our cries for help
so much faster than we could before

but what if we don't want to communicate
or forget how
too busy leaving messages, voice mails,
emails, pager numbers
forgetting to call back

what if we forget
how to communicate

VI

i wanted to purchase tickets for a concert
but i was shopping with my sister
and wasn't near a ticket outlet
but my sister said, "i have a portable phone,
you can call them if you'd like"
so she gave me the phone, and i looked
at all these extra buttons, and she said,
"just press the 'power' button, but hold it down
for at least four seconds, until the panel lights up,
then dial the number, but use the area code, because
this phone is a 630 area code, then press 'send'.
when you're done with the call, just press 'end', and
make sure the light turns off."

so i turned it on, dialed the number,
pressed 'send', pressed my head
against the tiny phone

and the line was busy
and i couldn't get through

VII

i wanted to get in touch
with an old friend of mine from high school,
vince, and the last i heard was that he went to
marquette university. well, that was five years ago, he
could be anywhere. i talked to a friend or two that
knew him, but they lost touch with him, too.
so i searched on the internet, to see
if his name was on a website or if
he had an email address. he didn't.
so i figured i probably wouldn't find him.
and all this time, i knew his parents lived
in the same house they always did, i could just
look up his parent's phone number in the phone book,
and call them, say i'm an old high school friend
of vince's, but i never did. and then i realized why.

you see, i could search the internet for hours
and no one would know that i was looking for someone.
but now, with a single phone call, i'd make it known
to his family that i wanted to see him enough to call,
after all these years. and i didn't want
him to know that. so i never called.

VIII

now that we have the information superhighway
we can throw out into the open
our screams
our cries for help
so much faster than we could before

but then the question begs itself:
who
is there
to listen

You Have No Idea

a recent poem Janet Kuypers wrote,
written in the Summer of 2020

we try to understand the details
we research, we study the core of the matter
and we believe we understand it all...

until we find out that we're missing
pieces; we're only seeing a tiny fraction of what
makes things work the way they do

#

astrophysicists & science philosophers
have tried to unravel the key to the Universe
and only now speculate a theory...

& these science types *live* on theories
I mean, that's why we call it the Big Bang *Theory*
we may have evidence, but no proof

so in this effort to understand
why the pieces don't all seem to fit into place
they make a theory they can't know:

for if something controls the physics,
controlling things in ways we don't understand,
maybe we're not meant to see

what controls it all

#

if there is something
these science types don't understand
the don't turn to a god

for it's their thing to come up
with theories they can try to prove or disprove —
so they came up with *Dark Matter*

they research & look for evidence
so they can hypothesize about this magical stuff,
this theoretical stuff we can't see...

and the only way they could find proof
is if *in* their experiments they found *nothing*
because a lack of *anything*

is the nature *of* their theory —
for it's impossible to even *see* their Dark Matter
"theory" in the first place

so after all this guesswork,
if things *still* don't make enough sense to them,
they hypothesize *then* about

something called *Dark Energy* —
something else they can never actually prove —
maybe, they think, maybe this

impossible theory number two
is the force driving everything in the Universe
apart　　*that* would make sense

#

look at these puzzles, look
at the preposterous nature of the lack
of a preponderance of evidence

and imagine that *this* is how
these science types formulate theories
the rest of us are supposed to

blindly believe

#

you think you know me
you see the pieces I spoon-feed you
you say you understand

but you have no idea

Under The Sea

the oldest poem
Janet Kuypers ever wrote,
in the Spring of 1980:

I'd like to be
Under the sea
To see the fish go swim,
I'd like to squish
A jelly fish
And then let go of him.
I'd like to grab
A soft-shelled crab
And take him for a walk
I'd like to hurdle
Over a turtle
And teach dolphins to talk.
I'd like to see
A manatee
And then go play by him,
I'd like to do
All of these things
If only I could swim!

www.ingramcontent.com/pod-product-compliance
Lightning Source LLC
Chambersburg PA
CBHW020721160726
47993CB00006B/2298